I Took
My Mommy's Heart
to School

Written by Roseanne Oppmann
Illustrated by Maria Ciaccio

AuthorHouse™
1663 Liberty Drive
Bloomington, IN 47403
www.authorhouse.com
Phone: 833-262-8899

Because of the dynamic nature of the Internet, any web addresses or links contained in this book may have changed
since publication and may no longer be valid. The views expressed in this work are solely those of the author and do
not necessarily reflect the views of the publisher, and the publisher hereby disclaims any responsibility for them.

Any people depicted in stock imagery provided by Getty Images are models,
and such images are being used for illustrative purposes only.
Certain stock imagery © Getty Images.

This book is printed on acid-free paper.

ISBN: 978-1-4969-5686-6 (hc)
ISBN: 978-1-4969-0805-6 (sc)
ISBN: 978-1-4918-5227-9 (e)

Library of Congress Control Number: 2014905840

Print information available on the last page.

Published by AuthorHouse 02/03/2021

authorHOUSE®

This book is dedicated to my wonderful
family, and to all of the children, teachers,
parents and dear friends who have given
me the inspiration and encouragement to
write this book.

One bright and sunny day, Myla and her mother got ready to go to the park. Myla loved to go to the park with her mother because they always had a lot of fun. It was a special time for them, and one of her favorite things to do.

She loved to run and play and she would twirl around, hopping, and jumping all the way to the swings. Her mother would run after her and Myla would jump on a swing, and her mother would push it just right--not too high, and not too fast.

On the way home, her mother would always point to the big school building near the park and say, "There's the school that you will go to someday." Myla would stare at the big building and wonder what school would be like.

Today, Myla thought about starting school tomorrow. "Mommy, will you still come and play with me at the park when I go to school?" she asked. Her Mommy said, "Of course we can still go to the park, but not when you are in school, you'll have lots of puppies to play with and you will learn exciting new things."

Myla kept thinking about school. She liked the way things were now and really didn't want them to change. That night she got out of bed several times. "Can I please have a drink of water, Daddy?" she asked. "Sure, but then you have to get some rest for your big day tomorrow," Daddy said.

After a while she got up again. "Mommy, Daddy, my tummy hurts, I don't feel so good," she said. "Oh, you're just excited about starting school tomorrow. You'll feel better in the morning," said her mother. Then they gave her a snuggle and a kiss and tucked her back into bed.

The next day, Myla was very quiet and hardly ate any breakfast. Myla's mother told her to hurry so they wouldn't be late on her first day of school. Myla said, "I don't think I want to go to school today. I don't feel very well. My head hurts and I feel sick."

Her mother smiled at her and said, "It's okay that you are feeling a little scared, everyone feels that way at times, but you have to go to school today." Then she took Myla's paw and said, "Come on, everything will be okay."

At school, everyone seemed very happy and excited, but Myla wasn't sure she wanted to be there. She held her mother's paw very tight and would not let go. She would not let go when the principal, Mr. Kirby, tried to talk to her.

She would not let go of her paw when the secretary told her she could
visit the office later. Or even when the teacher gave her a snuggle and
told her it would be okay. She just held her mother's paw and cried. "Please
let me go back home with you, Mommy."

Myla's mother looked very sad. The teacher told her not to worry because there was a special lady at school named Miss Lola. She was very good at helping puppies that were afraid to go to school. Myla could see that her mother really didn't want to go, so she cried even louder. "Please take me home Mommy."

Myla's mother said, "I am leaving now, I promise I will be back after school. I love you very much." Then she gave Myla a snuggle and a kiss and walked away, looking very sad. Myla cried, "Please don't go, Mommy. I'll miss you and Daddy too much."

Miss Lola

The teacher took Myla to Miss Lola's office. Miss Lola asked Myla if she wanted to sit in her special rocking chair. Myla sat down. Miss Lola told her that her job was to help all the puppies in the school, and that school was a fun place to learn new things. Myla cried, "But I want to do things with my Mommy, like go to the park. I'll miss her too much if I'm at school."

Miss Lola said softy, "Your mommy is here." Myla's eyes opened wide. "Is she in the office?" Miss Lola said, "No, she's in your heart, and she's always with you." Then she took Myla's paw and placed it on Myla's heart, and said, "We always have the ones we love in our hearts. When you think of your mommy just touch your heart and feel her with you." Myla stopped crying and smiled at Miss Lola and gave her a big snuggle.

Miss Lola took Myla to classroom 29, and Myla had fun the rest of the day. She met new puppies, played games, and learned new things.

Every once in a while she would put her paw over her heart and smile.

After school she told her mother and father all about what happened that day and what Miss Lola told her. Later that night just before bed, Myla's mother said "I have a surprise for you." and she handed her a box that was wrapped with beautiful red paper covered in hearts.

"What is it, Mommy?" she asked. "Open it up and see," said her mother. "It is something special for you to wear to school." Myla opened the box and saw two beautiful bracelets with the words *"IN MY HEART"* written on them.

Her mother took them out of the box and put one on Myla's paw and one on her own paw. "You can wear your bracelet to school to remind you that I am always with you, and I will wear my bracelet to remind you that you are always with me." Myla gave her mother a great big snuggle.

As her mother tucked Myla into bed she said, "I have something else for you. I wrote you a special poem that I hope you will always remember."

In My Heart You'll Always be

Whether the sun is shining or the clouds are gray,
in my heart you'll always stay

During the day or in the night,
I will hold you ever so tight

You never have to miss me, even while at school,
I want you to remember this one special rule.

My heart is always with you because I love you so,
no matter where you are my heart will surely go.

I am in your heart and in my heart you'll always be
Just touch your wristband, close your eyes and simply think of me.

Tips For Parents

- A week before school starts share positive experiences you had.
- Together create a "school routine" schedule that includes bedtime, wake up time, what to wear, making lunches, checking homework etc.
- Visit school with your child before the first day.
- Prepare for the first day of school by letting your child make choices about his or her breakfast, lunch, outfits, etc. the night before.
- Bring your child the first day to emphasize the importance of school.
- Trust that the school staff has your child's best interest and safety in mind.
- Believe that your child is capable of being successful.
- Visualize your child making several friends during their day.
- Cherish the memories and the strong bond you have made with your child.
- Understand the first day may be difficult, but it is an important step towards your child developing independence.
- Have confidence that your child will make good decisions.
- Recognize that your child might have challenging times at school, but with love and encouragement, they will develop healthy life skills.
- Encourage your child daily by celebrating accomplishments.
- Have daily conversations with your child about their school experiences.
- Make school an important part of your child's life by attending conferences, parent nights, and as many school programs as possible.
- Regularly communicate with your child's teacher to build a positive home and school relationship.

Tips for Teachers/Counselors/Social Workers

- Be mindful of the stressors the family is experiencing.
- Remind the parents that you are there to support them and their child.
- Practice patience and understanding.
- Lend a helping hand and a kind ear for a child that needs support.
- Embrace the special moments you spend with your students and parents.
- Smile each day because a smile goes a long way in a child's life.
- Remember every child is a precious person to someone.
- Establish open communication with parents.
- Encourage and celebrate your students' progress.

These tips were compiled by Brian Bakalar, M.A in counseling

SPECIAL FAMILIES WHO ARE ALWAYS IN OUR HEARTS!

Myla's Family:

Roseanne and Ewald Oppmann

Lola's Family:

Brian, Danielle, Bennett

and Eliana Bakalar

Kirby's Family:

Maria and Laila Caiccio,

and Kenneth Knight

ABOUT THE AUTHOR

Roseanne Oppmann's strong passion, dedication to helping others, and encouragement from teachers over the years inspired the conception of *I Took My Mommy's Heart To School*. Roseanne has a Master of Arts in Human Service Counseling degree and is a Licensed Clinical Professional Counselor. The character of Myla was inspired by her true-to-life companion Myla, a certified therapy Goldendoodle, who accompanies her to work in her private counseling and consulting practice. Roseanne's invaluable experience as a former special education teacher and school counselor and her partnership with Myla, have helped numerous children and their parents overcome anxiety and fears about going to school.

ABOUT THE ILLUSTRATOR

Maria Ciaccio, a mother, illustrator, and professional web designer resides in Chicago, Illinois. Her inspiration comes from her vast appreciation for the arts, and her sweet daughter, Laila. She looks forward to each morning that she sends her daughter to school with a reminder that her Mommy will always be in her heart.

To find out how to order additional books, bracelets, or to schedule a visit with Myla, please contact us at:
myfriendmyla.com

Love and Snuggles,

Myla

Printed in the United States
By Bookmasters